MEMOS IN MINUTES

Also by
JOSEPH C. MANCUSO, Ph.D.

Mastering Technical Writing
(Addison-Wesley Publishing Company, 1990. Now available from The Training Edge.)

Fundamentals of Business Writing
(American Management Association, 1992)

Technical Editing
(Prentice-Hall, Inc., 1992. Now available from The Training Edge.)

THE TRAINING EDGE

14232 Marsh Lane, Suite 410
Dallas, Texas 75234
(800) 572-3657
(214) 620-1667
FAX (214) 243-3340

MEMOS IN MINUTES

For Business Professionals

Published by The Training Edge
Dallas

First Edition

Library of Congress Catalog Card Number: 95-090941

Word for Windows 6 is a product of Microsoft Corporation.
Windows is a registered trademark of Microsoft Corporation.

T<small>HE</small>
T<small>RAINING</small>

Published by The Training Edge
14232 Marsh Lane, Suite 410
Dallas, Texas 75234
(800) 572-3657
(214) 620-1667
FAX (214) 243-3340

Printed in the United States of America

ISBN 0-9643750-2-8

DEDICATION

With love for my wife Kelli, who
- produced *Memos in Minutes*
- titled the book
- wrote most of the "power tools" sections
- edited copy, and
- worked with me nights, weekends, and vacations to develop this book

CONTENTS

CONTENTS

HOW TO USE *MEMOS IN MINUTES*

THE STEPS IN THE MEMO WRITING PROCESS AND WORD 6 POWER TOOLS

Memos in Minutes wants you to use this book as a guide when you write memos, and it wants you to start writing your best memos ever, NOW!

Memos in Minutes is not a textbook. It is a self-paced, skill-building handbook, designed to be "a quick and easy read."

Memos in Minutes encourages you to use a memo writing process, aided by WORD 6 "power tools." These "power tools"—commands embedded in WORD 6— accelerate you through the memo writing process. Within minutes, you will master each of these commands.

HOW TO USE *MEMOS IN MINUTES*

The following graphic shows the relationship of the "power tools" to the steps in the memo writing process:

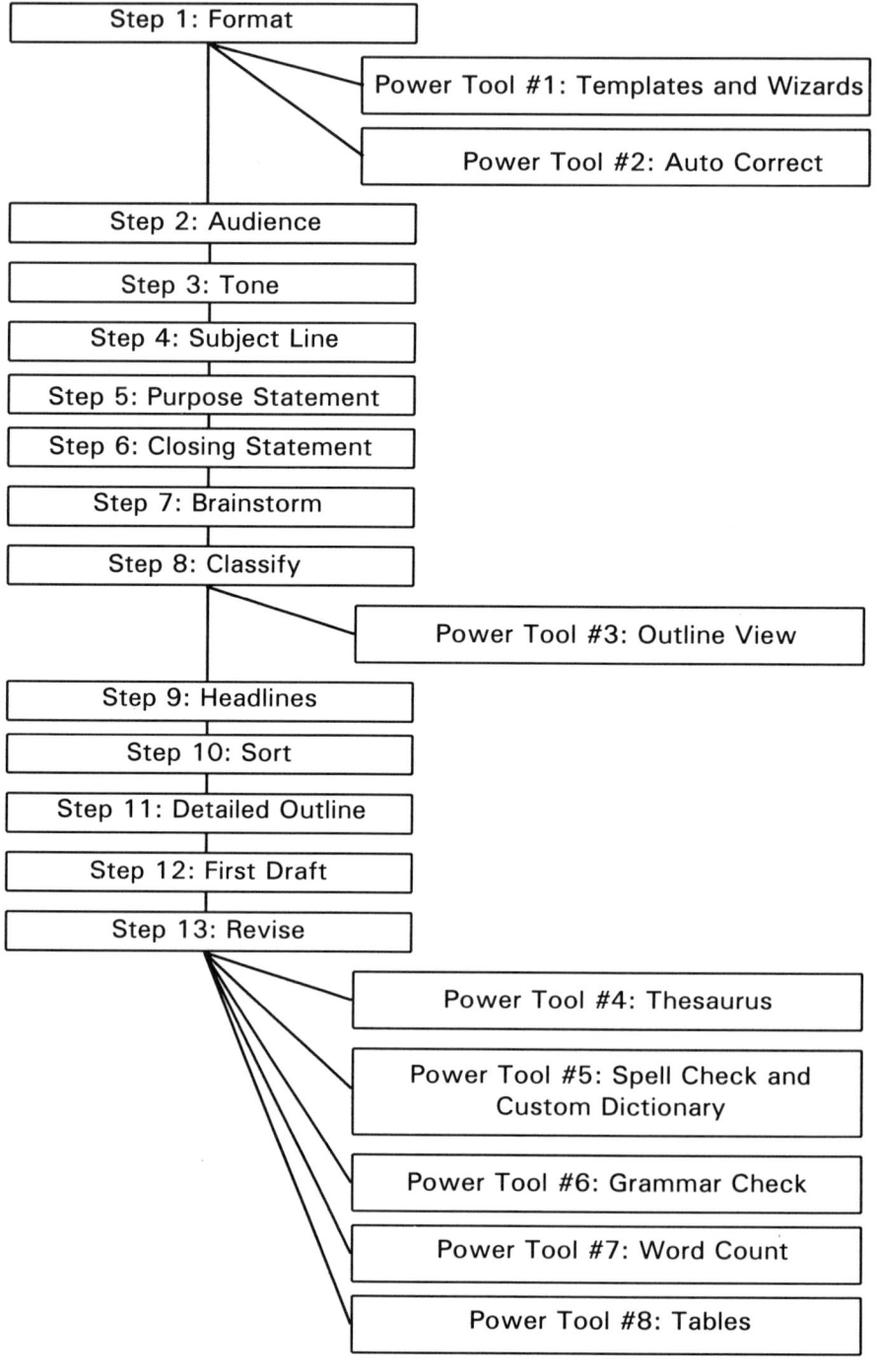

HOW TO USE *MEMOS IN MINUTES*

EACH STEP IN THE MEMO WRITING PROCESS CONTAINS PRINCIPLE, SAMPLE, AND ACTION SECTIONS

Each of the steps in the memo writing process begins with a *Principle* of memo writing. For example, *Step 1-Format* begins

> *Principle*   Formats display the elements of documents. For instance, memos contain the elements To, From, Subject, and Date. Letters contain a heading, inside address, salutation, body, complimentary close. Progress reports contain Work Accomplished and Work Yet to Be Done sections.

Each step then shows a *Sample*, or one way to apply the *Principle*.

Each *Sample* is one building block in a case study memo completed at the end of Step 13. The case study focuses on a problem in Kendra Corporation.

Here is the *Sample* in Step 1.

> *Sample*
>
> | MEMORANDUM |
> | --- |
> | Date: July 1, 19xx
To: John Smith, Proposal Manager
From: Allison Jones, Publications Supervisor
Subject: Conventions for Resumes Submitted with 1995 Kendra Corporation Proposals |

HOW TO USE *MEMOS IN MINUTES*

Each step in the memo writing process indicates **Actions** necessary to complete that step. Here are the actions required to complete Step 1.

Action Create a memo heading now. To do so, use **Power Tool #1-Templates and Wizards** on pages 17-19.

To minimize punctuation, capitalization, and typographical errors in a memo, use **Power Tool #2-Auto Correct** on page 21.

WRITE GREAT MEMOS AND OTHER BUSINESS DOCUMENTS, NOW

Memos in Minutes produces what it promises: tightly organized, clear, concise, appealing, and correct memos written in a fraction of the time.

Memos in Minutes stresses memo writing, but writers can apply the memo writing process and "power tools" to e-mail, letters, reports, and proposals.

ACKNOWLEDGMENTS

Many thanks to the following professionals for their help in evaluating and editing this manuscript:

Jim Lacy, Professional Engineer, author of *Systems Engineering Management: Achieving Total Quality*.

Leslie Kelly, Editor-in-Chief, *The ASTD Technical and Skills Training Handbook* (McGraw-Hill, Inc.)

Nita Thornton, Training and Organizational Development Manager, Mervyn's.

Jane Drake, freelance editor/writer.

STEP 1. FORMAT

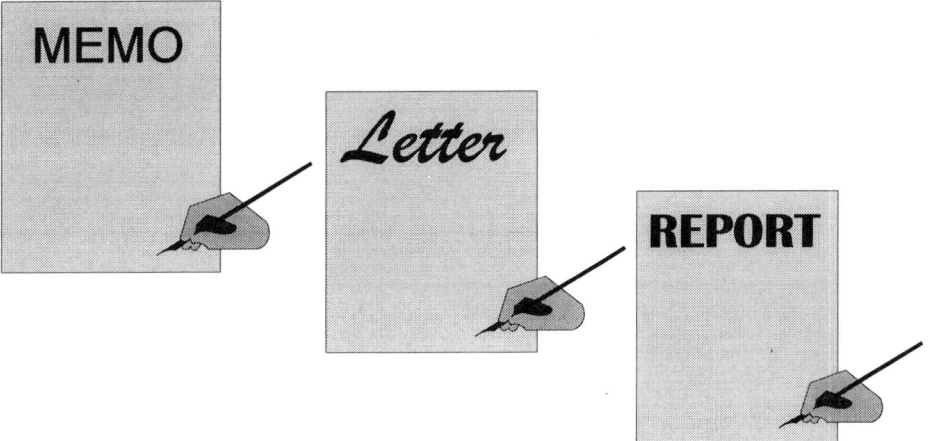

Principle Formats display the elements of documents. For instance, memos contain the elements To, From, Subject, and Date. Letters contain a heading, inside address, salutation, body, complimentary close. Progress reports contain Work Accomplished and Work Yet to Be Done sections.

15

Sample   The following memo heading identifies John Smith and Allison Jones of Kendra Corporation who will help solve Kendra's resume writing problem.

MEMORANDUM

Date: July 1, 19xx
To: John Smith, Proposal Manager
From: Allison Jones, Publications Supervisor
Subject: Conventions for Resumes Submitted with 1995 Kendra Corporation Proposals

---

Action   Create a memo heading now. Use ***Power Tool #1-Templates and Wizards*** on pages 17-19.

To minimize punctuation, capitalization, and typographical errors in a memo, use ***Power Tool #2-Auto Correct*** on page 21.

POWER TOOL #1
TEMPLATES and WIZARDS

Templates are pre-formatted documents that come with WORD software. Wizards customize and enhance templates by stepping writers through features not available in templates. Wizards ask users to type information that Wizards "crunch" into the format and then display.

To view templates and wizards:

1. Double-click on the MICROSOFT WORD icon in Program Manager.

2. Click on **File - New**.

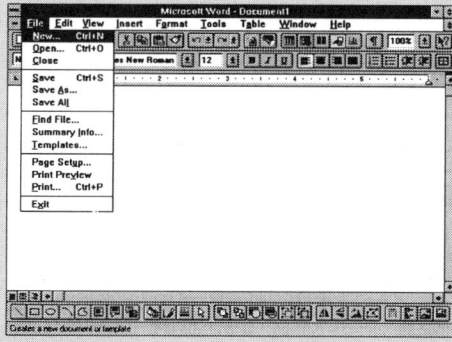

3. In the New dialog box, templates and wizards are combined. Scroll down the list of templates. Click on **Memo Wizard**, then click **OK**.

The Memo Wizard sets up the memo heading, the appropriate memo style, and headers and footers for multi-page memos.

> **NOTE**: *You may change your mind about selections you make in Memo Wizard. Click on* **Back** *to revert to previous dialog boxes and then make your changes.*
>
> *You may click* **Cancel** *in any dialog box, which will destroy your selections and take you back to your original document window.*
>
> *You may click* **Finish** *at any time. This will cause the Memo Wizard to create your memo using the most recent selections.*

4. The first Memo Wizard dialog box asks if you want to include a heading in your memo:

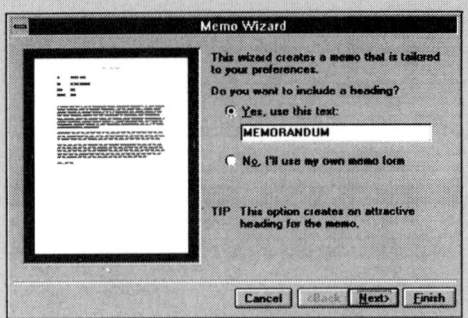

Click **Yes**, then type your heading, or use the default heading. Click on **Next** (at the bottom of the screen) to go to the next box.

5. The next dialog box asks if you want a separate page for your distribution list:

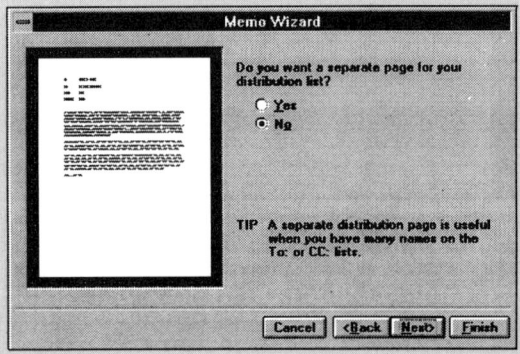

Click on **Yes** if your "To" or "CC" list is very long. Click on **No** if your memo is to be sent to one or a few people.

6. Click on **Next**. The next dialog box asks about specific items you want included in your memo:

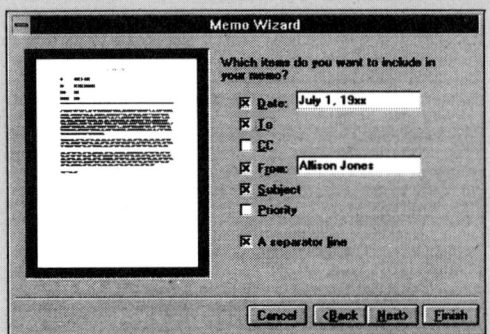

Click to mark an "x" in each box that is appropriate. Memo Wizard fills in the **From** box with the name of the person to whom the software is licensed. Click in the box to type a different name.

A separator line adds appeal to your memo by drawing a horizontal line between the addressing information and the body text of the memo.

7. Click on **Next**. The next dialog box asks if you want initials, enclosures, or attachments noted in your memo:

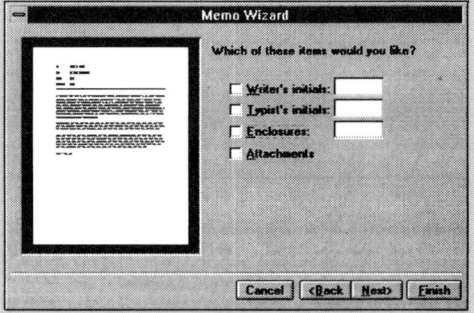

Click to mark an "x" in the appropriate boxes, then type initials or enclosures if applicable.

8. Click on **Next**. The next dialog box asks for items you want included in the header and/or footer of your memo:

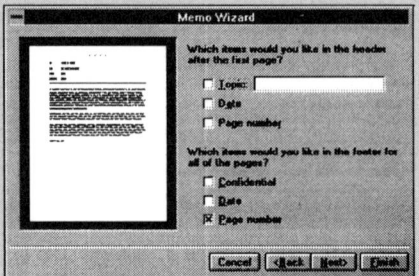

If your memo will not be longer than one page, you may leave the header question blank. The footer information will appear even on a one-page memo, so click to put an "x" in any or all of the appropriate footer options.

9. Click on **Next**. The next dialog box offers 3 memo format styles.

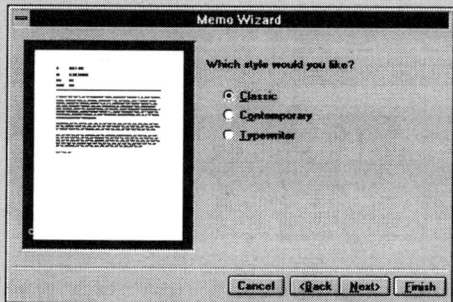

Click in each of the answers, and watch the sample document box in the left portion of the dialog box. The sample document layout will reflect the chosen style.

10. Click on **Next**. The final dialog box asks if you want Help displayed as you work:

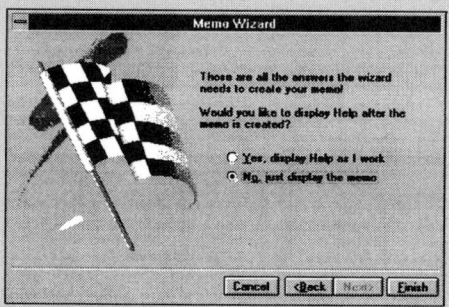

Click on **No**. Then, click on **Finish**, and your new memo heading is displayed on the screen.

11. Type the **To** line at the top of the memo to complete the heading.

WORD has typed your memo heading in Normal View, the screen you see whenever you open WORD 6. Keep the heading in Normal View for now. Leave the subject line blank. You will complete that part in Step 4 of the memo writing process.

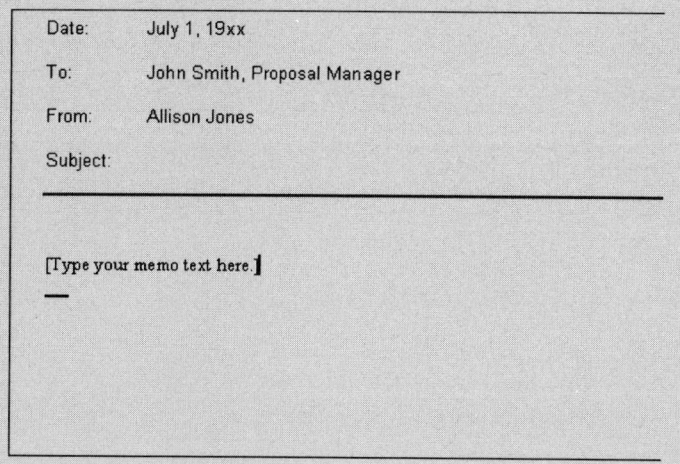

If for some reason, your screen is not in Normal View, click **View** on the Menu Bar, then click **Normal**.

POWER TOOL #2
AUTO CORRECT

Auto Correct will automatically correct many common errors as you type. It will

1) Change straight quotes (") to smart quotes (")
2) Correct two initial capitals
3) Capitalize the first letter of sentences
4) Capitalize names of days
5) Replace text as you type

Auto Correct, like Spell Check and Custom Dictionary, is a power tool individual writers can customize to fit their special circumstances.

1. Click on **Tools - Auto Correct**.

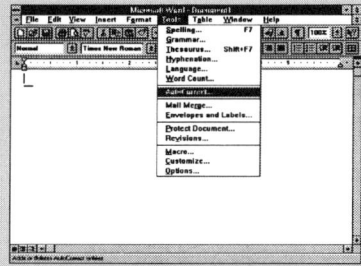

2. Look at each option and decide if you really want WORD to make these decisions for you.

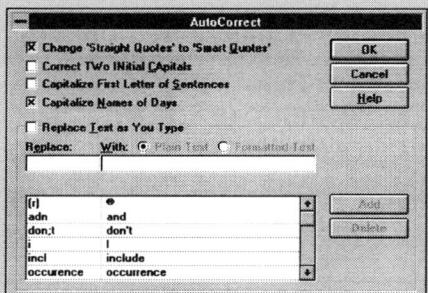

The Auto Correct tool is handy, but it can "drive you crazy" by changing text you may not want changed. Consider each option carefully when deciding which Auto Correct features to activate:

A. Straight quotes vs. smart quotes. Smart quotes are appropriate for enclosing dialogue, for example, "John, come here." Use straight quotes with numbers to denote linear measurements such as feet and inches, for example, 2'3". Deactivate smart quotes if you use straight quotes frequently.

B. Correct two initial capitals. This feature is handy 95% of the time, so you should probably leave it activated. You will want to deactivate it if you work at a company like Texas Instruments, which refers to its employees as "TIers."

C. Capitalize first letter of sentences. This is handy, unless you use many abbreviations. This option, when activated, will insert a capital letter after every period that is typed. It would change "Acme Co. reported today" to "Acme Co. Reported today." Most users will want to deactivate this feature.

D. Capitalize names of days. Sure, why not?

E. Replace text as you type. Scroll down the list of automatic replacements to become familiar with them. Some are good; some are not so good. For instance, you will not want WORD to replace "(r)" with "®," or "(i)" with "(I)." Either deactivate this feature completely to avoid all replacements, or delete those individual replacements that may cause you problems. You may also add replacement features.

STEP 2. AUDIENCE

Principle Writers should ask, "Who is my audience? What are its requirements? How do I convey my message so that my audience will understand?" Does it make sense to prepare a two-hour presentation in English and discover that the audience speaks and understands only Japanese? Or, write a memo to an audience of laypersons using jargon?

Examples   <u>Audience Requirements and Writing Techniques</u>

The example below lists some of the needs or requirements of certain audiences. The example also shows techniques which writers use to satisfy requirements.

AUDIENCE	*REQUIREMENTS*	*WRITING TECHNIQUES*
Executives	Analyze trends, set company policy	Clear and concise writing style, summaries
Managers	Make decisions, carry out policy	Background material, necessary facts, comparisons and contrasts, justifications, descriptions
	Distribute/present information to others	Lists (vertical, linear)
	Need information about human and raw resources	Accurate information, tables, graphs, footnotes
	Need information presented succinctly	One-page memo, overviews, summaries, glossaries
Experts	Become familiar with research	Hypotheses, methods, results; jargon
Customers	Need to be educated about products, services	Definitions, examples, theme statements
Editors	Circulate the manuscript	Multiple copies, required number of pages
Multiple Audience (e.g., experts and laypersons)	Easily understood by all levels	Glossaries, footnotes, separate sections
Technicians	Repair, maintain equipment	Imperative mood for procedures, drawings, photos, cerlox bind

Examples   <u>Document Requirements and Writing Techniques</u>

In addition to audiences, individual documents impose requirements on writers. The following example shows some of these requirements and the techniques writers use to satisfy them.

DOCUMENT	*REQUIREMENTS*	*WRITING TECHNIQUES*
Memos	Briefly inform superiors, colleagues, and subordinates about past, pending, and future business	Appropriate headings; clear, concise writing style; headlines; appropriate tone
Progress Reports	Inform superiors, colleagues, subordinates about the status of a project	Bulleted and enumerated lists; clear, concise writing style; headlines -- Work Accomplished, Work Yet To Be Done, Tasks, Deadlines
Annual Reports	Inform stockholders; contains a letter to stockholders from chief executive officer; present financial information	Charts, tables, photos, drawings; optimistic tone
Marketing Brochures	Pursuade customers	Photos, drawings, background/ history, data, features/benefits
Policy Statements	Inform full spectrum of employees	Middle range readability level (7th-9th grade), features/benefits

Sample   The following Sample identifies the audience for the Kendra Corporation case study memo. Note that the audience for the memo is Kendra's chief proposal manager, John Smith. This Sample table keeps the writer (Kendra's Allison Jones, a publications supervisor) on track as to her audience's and the document's requirements.

AUDIENCE / DOCUMENT	REQUIREMENTS	WRITING TECHNIQUES
Chief Proposal Manager	Makes decisions, carries out policy	Background material, necessary facts, comparisons and contrasts, descriptions
	Distributes/presents information to others	Lists (vertical, linear)
	Needs information about human and raw resources	Accurate information, tables, graphs, footnotes
	Needs information presented succinctly	One-page memo, overviews, summaries, glossaries
Memo	Short, informative; analysis of company business	Appropriate headings; clear, concise writing style; headlines, accurate information

Action   Create a table to prompt you as you write a memo. Pattern the table after the one in the above Sample.

—Notes—

STEP 3. TONE

Principle   When business professionals actually speak to audiences, they use their voices to sound gentle, firm, or playful; their voices reinforce the content of the message.

When business professionals write to audiences, they use words, punctuation, and highlighting techniques to reinforce their messages.

Tone is the atmosphere, or mood, writers achieve as they communicate their written messages.

Kinds of Tone

Formal	Complimentary
Informal	Friendly
Humorous	Diplomatic
Ironic	Firm
Solicitous	Constructive

Examples   <u>Different Tones</u>

- *Jim, I'll bring the books over in a few days—after I get them from the publisher. Can you imagine the guy taking that long to ship a few boxes of books?* (Informal tone)

- *Mr. Lemon, I will deliver the books by September 3 after I receive them from Wister Publishing. I apologize for the delay, but Wister has taken weeks to ship the books.* (Formal tone)

- *Unless you ship the promised books to me by August 29 so that I can deliver them to Mr. Lemon by September 3, I will find a more reliable publisher.* (Firm tone)

- *I want to continue to do business with you, but shouldn't you be checking with your shipping department? You were supposed to send me fifty copies of <u>Business Reports</u> by August 1, and here it is August 17. I have heard nothing from your shipping department or from your marketing department with whom I placed the order. Are your departments communicating with each other? They are not communicating with customers.* (Constructive tone)

Sample The Kendra Corporation Sample memo will set a formal, informative tone. The memo should

1) Be free from <u>accusations</u> of negligence and ignorance

2) <u>Suggest</u> successful resume-writing conventions to convey important information about company personnel

3) <u>Respectfully request</u> that John Smith, Kendra's chief proposal manager, broadcast the resume-writing conventions to proposal writers and project personnel

4) <u>Offer help</u> in disseminating resume-writing conventions by presenting the information at kickoff meetings.

Words and phrases like *offer, suggest, advise, experience, successful, communicative,* and *innovative* can reinforce the proper tone for the memo.

Action Prepare notes to prompt the creation of an appropriate tone throughout a memo. Pattern the notes after the above Sample.

—Notes—

STEP 4. SUBJECT LINE

Subject

Principle Writers place a subject line in the heading of a memo. Subject lines forecast the contents of memos. They help audiences to read memos more intelligently. Writers should express subject lines in initial capitals.

Examples **Subject Lines**

- *An Evaluation of the "Conducting Effective Oral Presentations" Course*

- *1995 Roster of Management Trainee Courses*

- *1996-97 Marketing Strategies for the Financial Assistance Program*

- *Price List for Desktop Publishing Services (Newsletters, Brochures, Advertising Copy)*

- *Problems Discovered on the Restan Project*

Sample

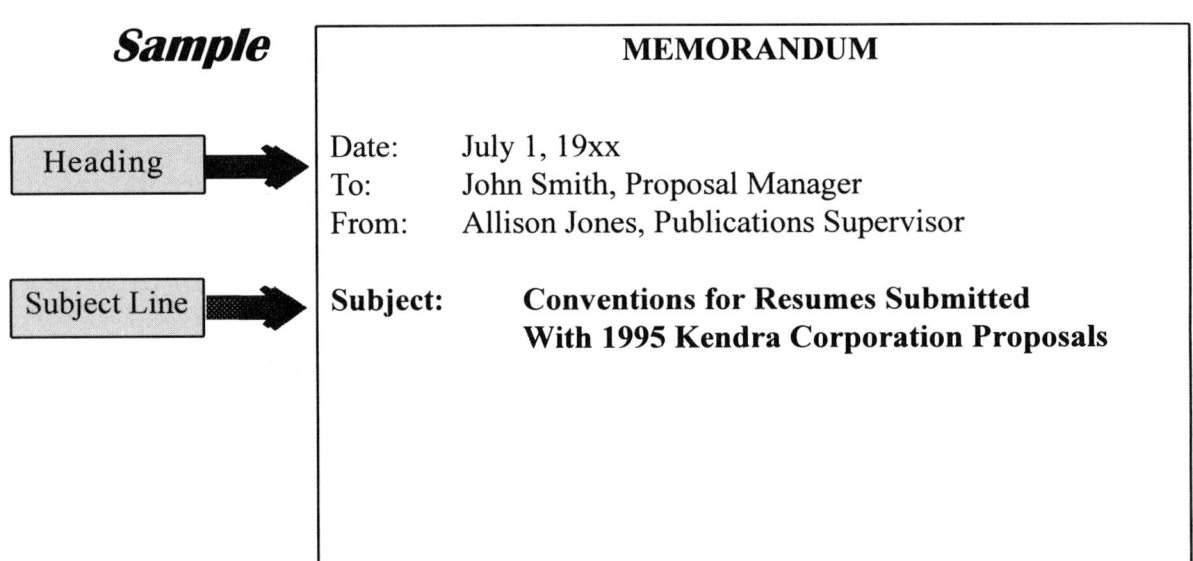

Action Add a subject line in initial capitals to a memo heading. (Your computer screen should be in WORD's Normal View when you add the subject line.)

STEP 5. PURPOSE STATEMENT

Principle Purpose statements tell audiences why writers communicate information. Without a purpose statement, audiences don't know why they read information writers disclose.

To develop a purpose statement, writers must answer two questions:

> **1.** What kind of information am I offering?

> **2.** Why am I offering this information?

Examples Purpose Statements

- *This memo discusses reasons for SellTech purchasing the "Conducting Effective Oral Presentations" course from Poseidon Corporation.*

- *This memo contains the 1995 Roster of Management Trainee Courses so that you and other team members may complete training requirements for 1995.*

- *SellTech executives will team with the three companies mentioned in this memo to develop marketing strategies for the International Semiconductor Consortium.*

- *Consult the enclosed "Price List for Desktop Publishing" for any work planned for Third Quarter 1995.*

Sample

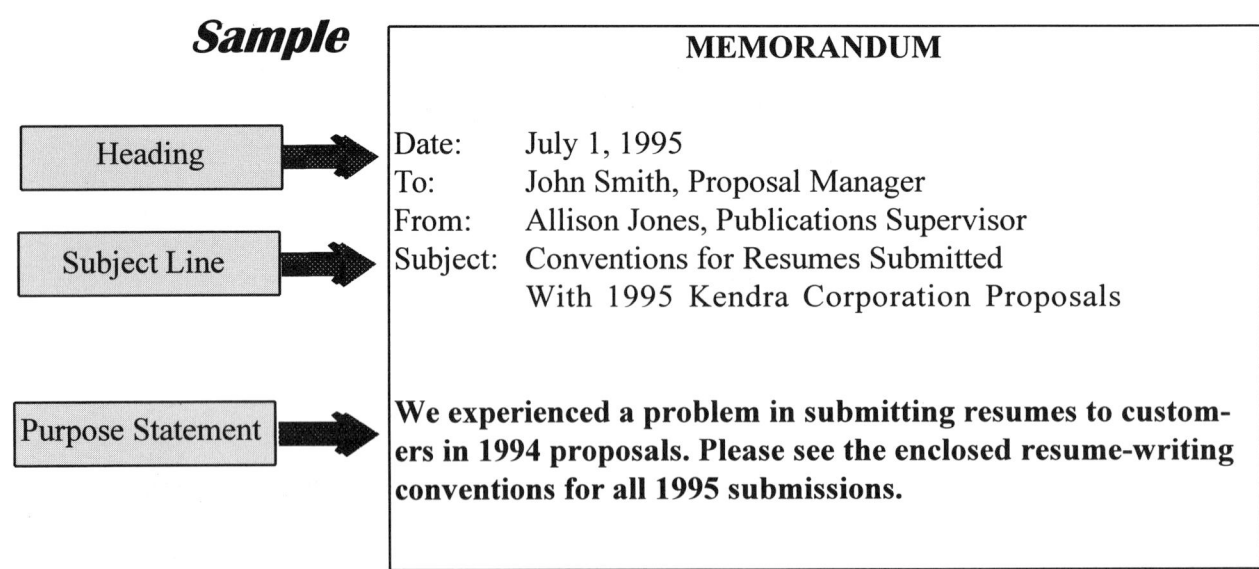

MEMORANDUM

Date: July 1, 1995
To: John Smith, Proposal Manager
From: Allison Jones, Publications Supervisor
Subject: Conventions for Resumes Submitted
           With 1995 Kendra Corporation Proposals

We experienced a problem in submitting resumes to customers in 1994 proposals. Please see the enclosed resume-writing conventions for all 1995 submissions.

Heading

Subject Line

Purpose Statement

Action   Add a purpose statement to the first paragraph of a memo. Use as many sentences as you need.

STEP 6. CLOSING STATEMENT

Principle   Closing statements encourage action
from audiences by telling audiences what
they can do to accomplish the business
discussed in memos. In formulating
closing statements, writers should ask
themselves, "What is the audience supposed to do with, or about, my message—and by when?"

Writers express their closing statements
in a facilitative, motivating tone, and
place them in the document's last paragraph.

Writers should develop closing statements at the beginning of the memo
writing process to keep the memo's body
text "on track" from the outset.

Examples <u>Closing Statements</u>

- *Please bring all materials discussed in this memo to the meeting on August 8, 1995 at 4:00 P.M. in Conference Room 5G.*

- *Distribute the enclosed brochure to members of your team.*

- *Address your check or money order to <u>Living Well</u>, and mail before midnight October 6, 1995 to take advantage of this offer.*

- *Please study the proposed purchase plan, and comment on its advantages and disadvantages.*

- *Return the product within three weeks for a full refund of your purchase price.*

Sample

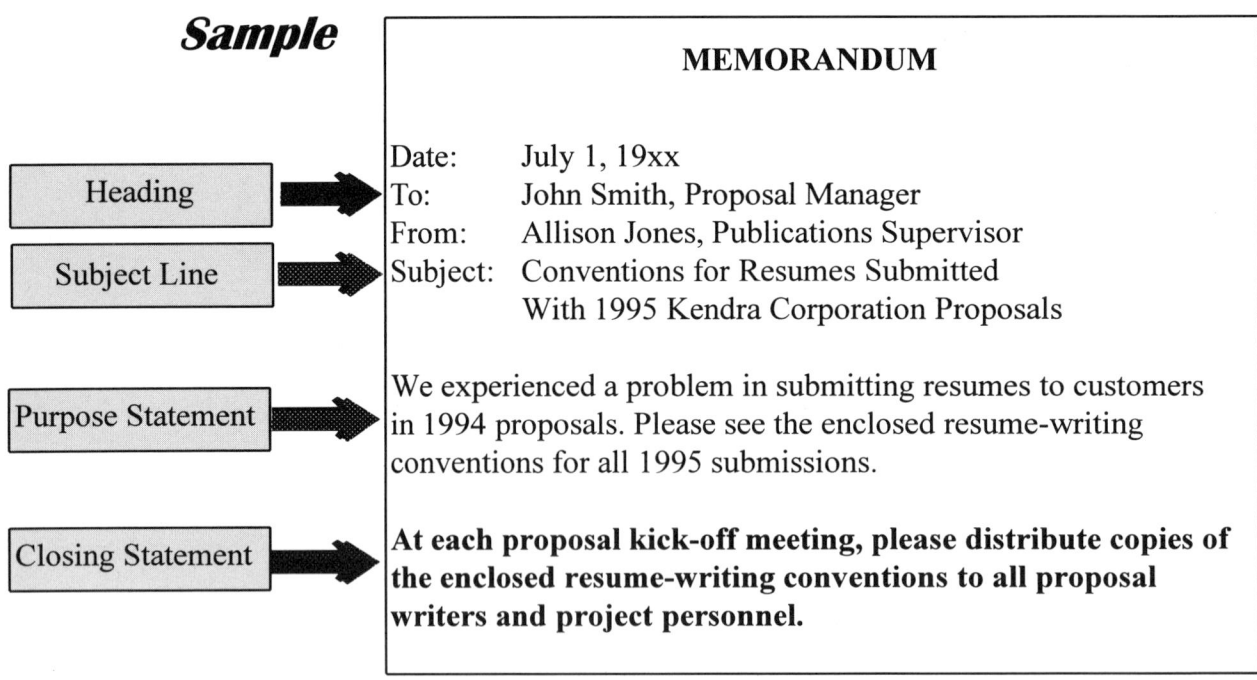

Heading →

Subject Line →

Purpose Statement →

Closing Statement →

MEMORANDUM

Date: July 1, 19xx
To: John Smith, Proposal Manager
From: Allison Jones, Publications Supervisor
Subject: Conventions for Resumes Submitted
            With 1995 Kendra Corporation Proposals

We experienced a problem in submitting resumes to customers in 1994 proposals. Please see the enclosed resume-writing conventions for all 1995 submissions.

At each proposal kick-off meeting, please distribute copies of the enclosed resume-writing conventions to all proposal writers and project personnel.

Action

After writing a purpose statement, add a closing statement to the memo with the understanding that you will insert body text between these two statements in *Step 7-Brainstorm*.

STEP 7. BRAINSTORM

Principle Brainstorming triggers the outflow of ideas a writer will use in the body of a memo. Brainstorming is a "brain dump" for the author's eyes only.

In brainstorming, writers

1. Capture all ideas associated with a subject without evaluating the ideas

2. Express these ideas as words, fragments, complete thoughts, abbreviations, "creatively" spelled words, ungrammatical constructions, etc.

3. Do not stop to correct text; they save that work for the revising step.

Sample

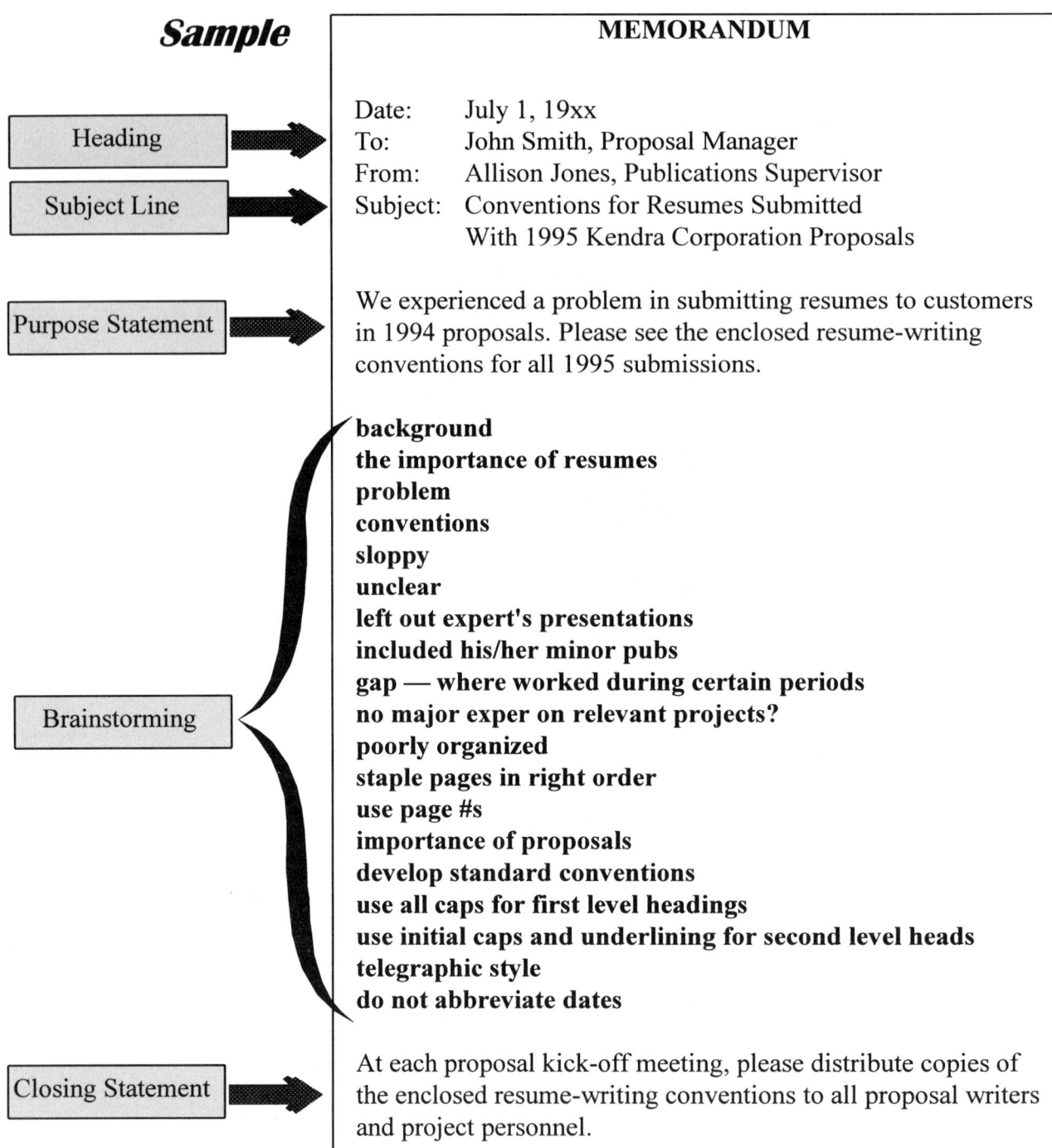

MEMORANDUM

Heading ➤

Subject Line ➤

Date: July 1, 19xx
To: John Smith, Proposal Manager
From: Allison Jones, Publications Supervisor
Subject: Conventions for Resumes Submitted
           With 1995 Kendra Corporation Proposals

Purpose Statement ➤

We experienced a problem in submitting resumes to customers in 1994 proposals. Please see the enclosed resume-writing conventions for all 1995 submissions.

Brainstorming

**background
the importance of resumes
problem
conventions
sloppy
unclear
left out expert's presentations
included his/her minor pubs
gap — where worked during certain periods
no major exper on relevant projects?
poorly organized
staple pages in right order
use page #s
importance of proposals
develop standard conventions
use all caps for first level headings
use initial caps and underlining for second level heads
telegraphic style
do not abbreviate dates**

Closing Statement ➤

At each proposal kick-off meeting, please distribute copies of the enclosed resume-writing conventions to all proposal writers and project personnel.

Action   Between the purpose statement and the closing statement, insert a brainstorming section filled with preliminary ideas for a memo. (Remember, you are writing all ideas in WORD's Normal View.)

STEP 8. CLASSIFY

Principle   In classifying, writers group brainstormed ideas into categories of similar information.

Writers may group ideas by numbering similar ideas. For instance, they mark all ideas in a "Background" category with the number "1." All ideas in a "Problem" category with "2." All ideas in a "Conventions" category with "3." And so on.

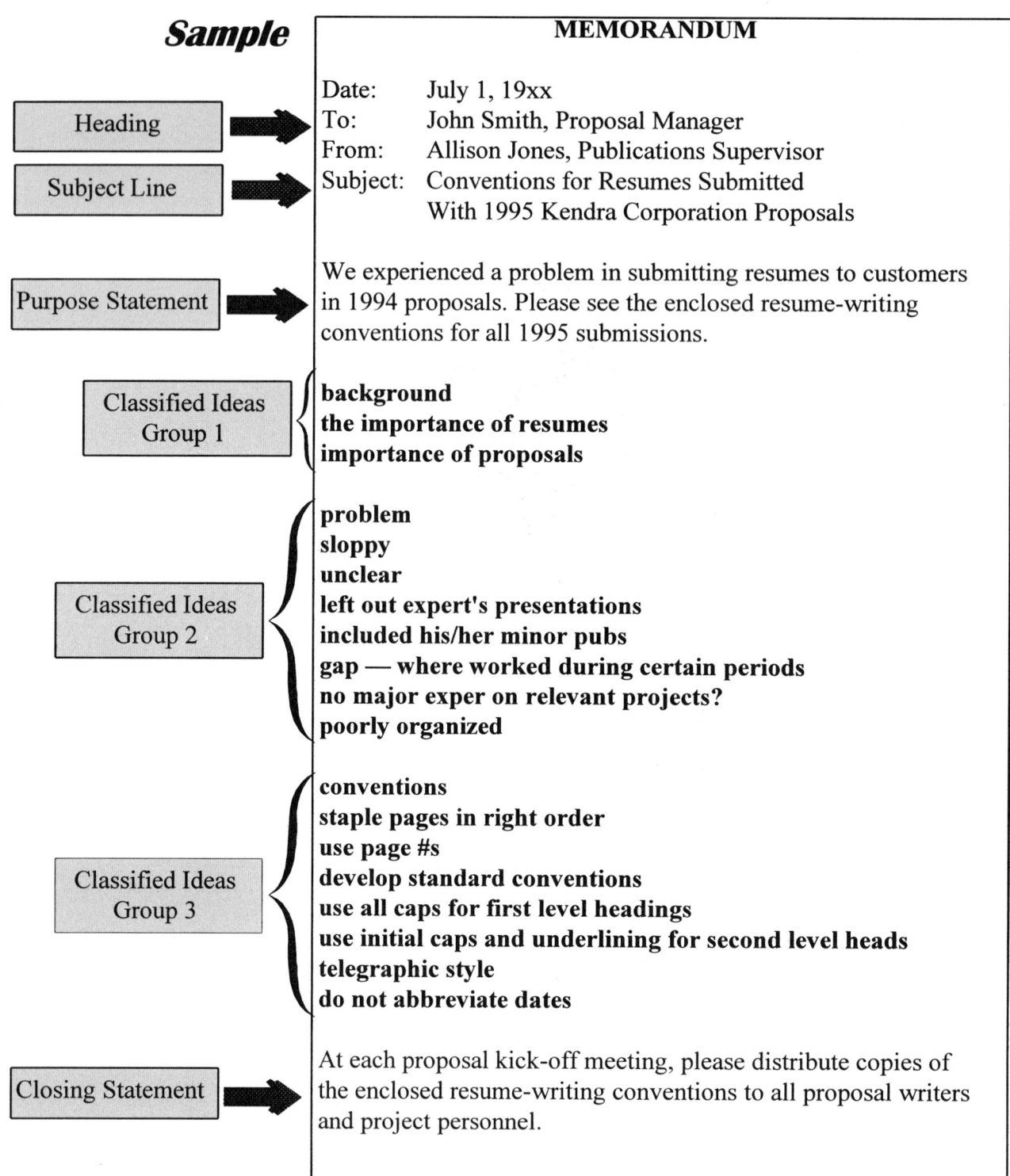

Sample

| Heading | → | MEMORANDUM |
| Subject Line | → | |

Date: July 1, 19xx
To: John Smith, Proposal Manager
From: Allison Jones, Publications Supervisor
Subject: Conventions for Resumes Submitted
           With 1995 Kendra Corporation Proposals

Purpose Statement →

We experienced a problem in submitting resumes to customers in 1994 proposals. Please see the enclosed resume-writing conventions for all 1995 submissions.

Classified Ideas Group 1

background
the importance of resumes
importance of proposals

Classified Ideas Group 2

problem
sloppy
unclear
left out expert's presentations
included his/her minor pubs
gap — where worked during certain periods
no major exper on relevant projects?
poorly organized

Classified Ideas Group 3

conventions
staple pages in right order
use page #s
develop standard conventions
use all caps for first level headings
use initial caps and underlining for second level heads
telegraphic style
do not abbreviate dates

Closing Statement →

At each proposal kick-off meeting, please distribute copies of the enclosed resume-writing conventions to all proposal writers and project personnel.

Action   You may classify brainstormed information manually, according to the directions under the *Principle* on page 43, or you may use *Power Tool #3-Outline View* on pages 45-46 to accomplish this. The author recommends your using *Power Tool #3*, one of the most helpful software tools you will ever use.

POWER TOOL #3
OUTLINE VIEW

Writers may categorize, sort, and outline the ideas they created in a brainstorming session by using WORD's Outline View (instructions 1, 2, and 3). Outline View allows writers to move information, promote it, and demote it much more quickly than in WORD's Normal View.

From this point on in the writing process, writers may work exclusively in Outline View, using it to create and shift new ideas efficiently.

How to Use the Outline View

1. Click on **View - Outline**.

This places you in Outline view in an active document window.

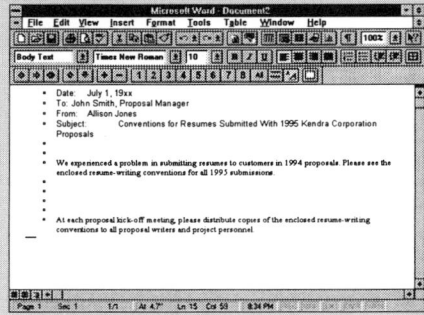

Note the Outline toolbar which replaces the ruler:

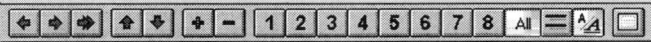

2. To move a line of text, place your cursor anywhere on the line of text to be moved, then click on one of two buttons on the Outline toolbar:

 Move Up button. Moves the selected line up.

 Move Down button. Moves the selected line down.

These two buttons should supply the help you need to categorize your brainstorming session.

3. To prioritize lines of text (see ***Step 10-Sort***), you may designate them as first-level headings, second-level headings, third-level headings, fourth-level headings, or body text. For example, to promote a line of text up a level, place your cursor on the line, go to the Outline toolbar, and click on the left arrow button.

 Promote button. Promotes the heading by one level.

To demote a line of text to a lower level, click on one of two buttons:

 Demote button. Demotes the line by one level.

 Demote to Body Text button. Demotes the line to body text.

Other Options in Outline View

The commands in this section show writers more ways to manipulate text while in Outline View.

(A) To view more of your detailed outline in the active document window, click the **First Line Only** button, a toggle switch, on the Outline toolbar.

This will cause the outline to display all headings and the first line of each paragraph.

Also click the **Show Formatting** button on the Outline toolbar to display all headings in body text format.

(B) After completing most or all of your detailed outline, you may wish to number it. To do so, click **Format** on the Menu Bar and then click **Heading Numbering**.

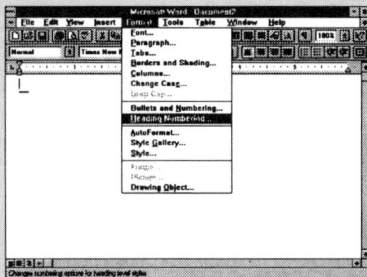

Heading Numbering will display 6 different numbering formats for you to choose from. Click on one of the formats and Outline view will automatically number sentences and ideas in the outline.

(C) If you wish to use your detailed outline as a table of contents for your document, click **Insert** on the Menu Bar and then click **Index and Tables**.

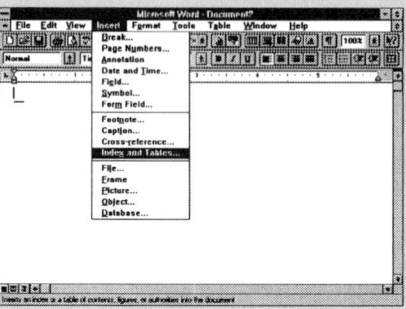

Next, click the tab marked **Table of Contents** and select desired options.

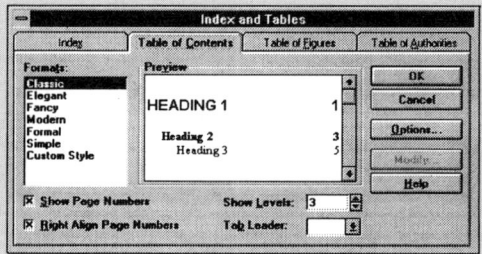

Click **OK**.

(D) To print your outline as seen in the Outline active document window, click **File** on the Menu Bar, then **Print**, then **OK**.

STEP 9. HEADLINES

EXTRA!!! The Times EXTRA!!!

Principle   A headline, placed just above the first line of a category (see ***Step 8-Classify***), is a string of words describing the information in a category. These strings may contain action verbs, company names, places, problems, and solutions.

Headlines act as mini-abstracts for categories and allow audiences to say, "Yes, I should read this information," or "No, I can skip these ideas because I already understand them."

Examples <u>Headlines</u>

- *The American Society of Training Managers Offers More Benefits Than Other Professional Organizations in the Communications Field*

- *Advantages of the TRX-479 Over the TRX-478*

- *Employees May Shelter Tax Dollars in Four Ways*

Sample

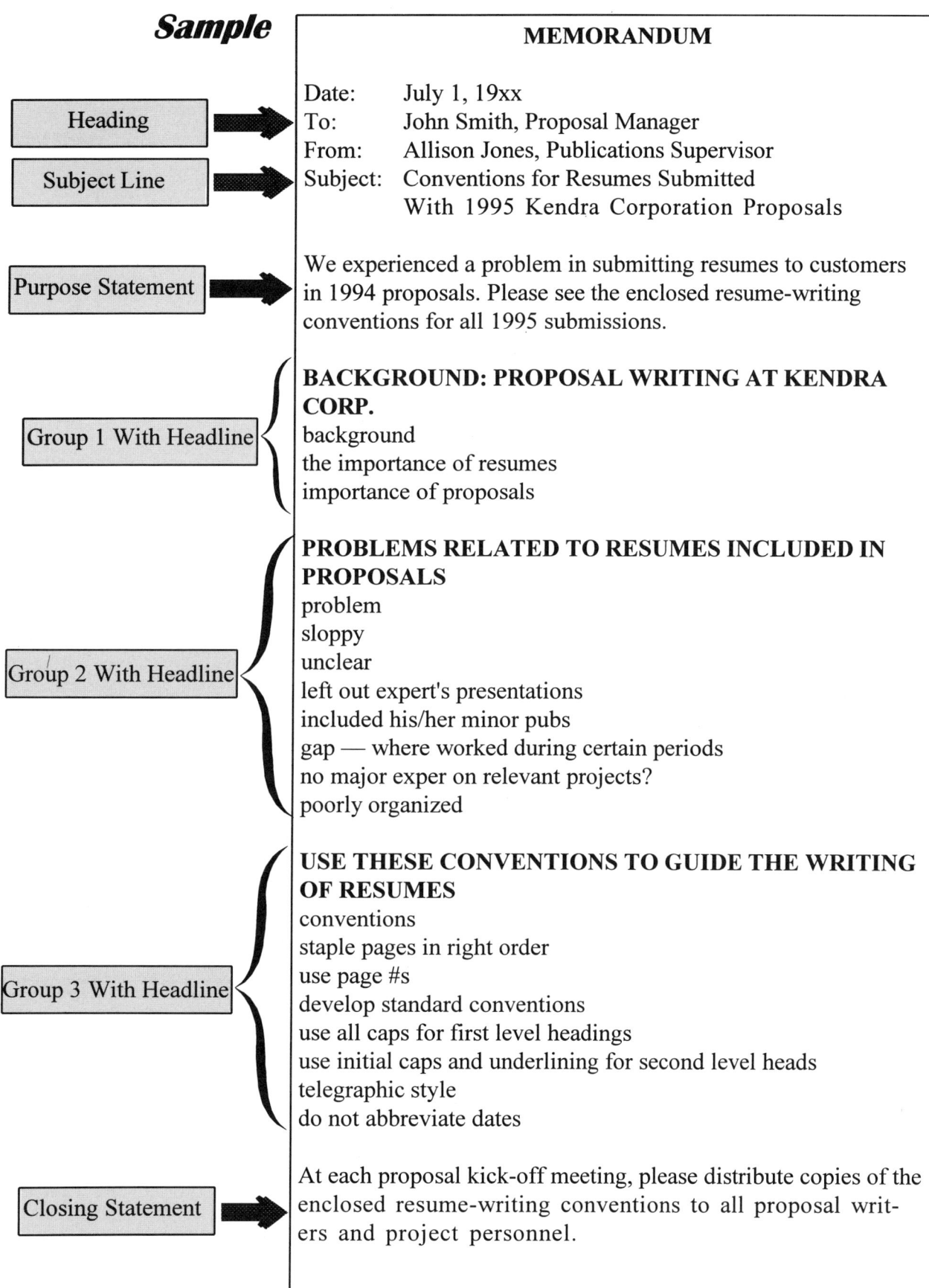

MEMORANDUM

Date: July 1, 19xx
To: John Smith, Proposal Manager
From: Allison Jones, Publications Supervisor
Subject: Conventions for Resumes Submitted
          With 1995 Kendra Corporation Proposals

We experienced a problem in submitting resumes to customers in 1994 proposals. Please see the enclosed resume-writing conventions for all 1995 submissions.

BACKGROUND: PROPOSAL WRITING AT KENDRA CORP.
background
the importance of resumes
importance of proposals

PROBLEMS RELATED TO RESUMES INCLUDED IN PROPOSALS
problem
sloppy
unclear
left out expert's presentations
included his/her minor pubs
gap — where worked during certain periods
no major exper on relevant projects?
poorly organized

USE THESE CONVENTIONS TO GUIDE THE WRITING OF RESUMES
conventions
staple pages in right order
use page #s
develop standard conventions
use all caps for first level headings
use initial caps and underlining for second level heads
telegraphic style
do not abbreviate dates

At each proposal kick-off meeting, please distribute copies of the enclosed resume-writing conventions to all proposal writers and project personnel.

Labels (left column):
- Heading
- Subject Line
- Purpose Statement
- Group 1 With Headline
- Group 2 With Headline
- Group 3 With Headline
- Closing Statement

Action Add a headline to each group of ideas in the memo. Be sure each headline forecasts the ideas in each category.

STEP 10. SORT

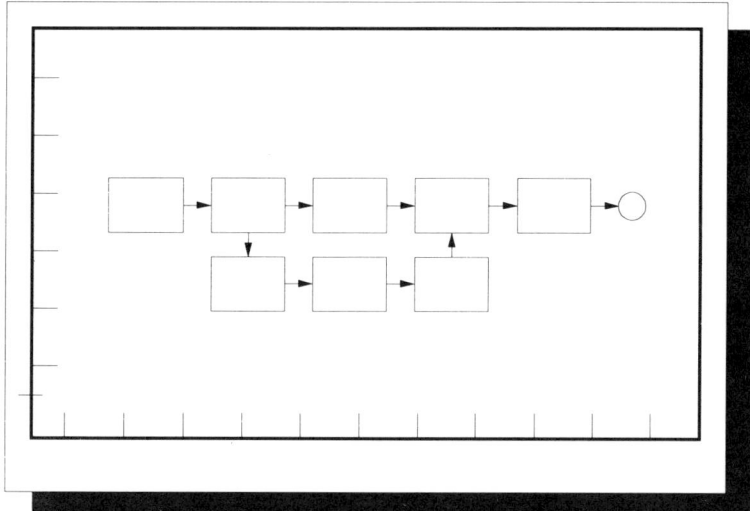

Principle In sorting, writers arrange text into logical patterns: for example—general to specific, chronological, most important to least important, spatial, comparison/ contrast, problem/solution. Other logical patterns exist. Those described below are the most popular ones.

Writers and audiences think logically. Hopefully, their sense of logic will mesh within the same document. A smooth logical flow allows audiences to absorb information quickly and thoroughly. Writers should never underestimate the power of a tight, logical arrangement of ideas.

General to Specific

Writers use the general to specific pattern, or reporting pattern, more often than any other. It reverses the writer's thinking pattern: with the thinking pattern, writers gather clues, and end with a general statement; in the reporting pattern, writers begin with a general statement, and follow with specifics. Hence, this pattern begins with a recommendation, conclusion, or hypothesis, and continues with support for the general statement.

Example

- *In the past three surveys, all three managers recommended the company raise salaries of editors. Inflation was skyrocketing, again. The perception of the importance of editors in the workplace had risen considerably. The pool of editors was shrinking.*

Chronological

When writers report progress to colleagues, they use the chronological pattern. They begin with the first event and continue to succeeding ones.

Example

- *We began developing the aircraft on January 2, 1990. We were racing Farnsworth in producing this technology. On January 23, the company learned that Farnsworth had also begun developing the same technology. On February 2, I submitted our report to upper level management...*

Most Important to Least Important

When writers know that audiences may not have time to read all their ideas, they use the most important to least important pattern. They present information in a descending order of importance so that audiences will at least read the most important ideas.

Example
- *The proposal manager described the outline writers should follow. The manager stipulated deadlines for the sections of the proposal. Proposal writing activity would center in the Wooded Creek complex. The Wooded Creek complex, located in the northern part of the city,...*

Spatial

When writers describe the contents of rooms or a particular view of a product, they use the spatial pattern. This pattern presents information from left to right, top to bottom, or near to far, depending on the needed perspective.

Example
- *The remodeled third floor of the office complex pleased the eye. The reception area was painted in a soothing light gray with a medium gray stripe bisecting all three walls. As I walked through the reception area to the inner offices, the color of the walls abruptly changed to burgundy — all business.*

Comparison/Contrast

When writers justify decisions for buying one product/ service over another, they use the comparison/contrast pattern. This pattern describes individual characteristics of products/services alternatively.

Example
- *Weight and cost are two of the most important factors in our decision to buy. Company A can build a prototype according to the required weight of 250 pounds. Company B's prototype will weigh 7 pounds more than the required weight. Company C can build the aircraft 11 pounds under the required weight. Company C's plane will cost $75,000 more than our stipulated cost. Company B's prototype will cost...*

Problem/Solution

When writers answer a request for a proposal, they use the problem/solution pattern. This pattern begins by defining the problem in the customer's terms and then follows with a solution.

Example

- *The Wings Corporation understands the Government's quandary. The Government needs an aircraft that military personnel can use in the field for flying short distances. Wings can supply that aircraft, incorporating the appropriate solution to the problem. Wings can develop an aircraft the average soldier can learn to fly in 5 hours. The aircraft is light for three soldiers to carry, and they can assemble it in 45 minutes.*

Sample

Heading →

Subject Line →

Purpose Statement →

Group 1 Sorted Into Problem/Solution Pattern {

Group 2 Sorted Into General to Specific Pattern {

Group 3 Sorted Into General to Specific Pattern {

Closing Statement →

MEMORANDUM

Date: July 1, 19xx
To: John Smith, Proposal Manager
From: Allison Jones, Publications Supervisor
Subject: Conventions for Resumes Submitted
          With 1995 Kendra Corporation Proposals

We experienced a problem in submitting resumes to customers in 1994 proposals. Please see the enclosed resume-writing conventions for all 1995 submissions.

BACKGROUND: PROPOSAL WRITING AT KENDRA CORP.
importance of well-written proposals
       importance of resumes

PROBLEMS RELATED TO RESUMES INCLUDED IN PROPOSALS
How these resume problems came to pubs' attention.
The kinds of problems pubs has observed in our company's resumes.
       unclear resumes
       poorly organized
       sloppy resumes
       no major exper on relevant projects?
       left out expert's presentations
            included his/her minor pubs
       gap — where worked during certain periods

USE THESE CONVENTIONS TO GUIDE THE WRITING OF RESUMES
Justification for using conventions all personnel in our company will follow.
Kinds of conventions necessary for our writers and experts to use.
       telegraphic style
       use all caps for first level headings
       use initial caps and underlining for second level heads
       use page #s
       do not abbreviate dates
       staple pages in right order

At each proposal kick-off meeting, please distribute copies of the enclosed resume-writing conventions to all proposal writers and project personnel.

Action   Use ***Power Tool #3-Outline View*** on pages 45-46 to move, promote, and demote information.

STEP 11. DETAILED OUTLINE

Principle   A detailed outline is a roadmap that describes the steps in a journey. Drawing a roadmap requires knowing the destination and directions, and communicating these clearly to travelers. For writers and audiences, "directions" take the form of formats, subject lines, closing statements, headlines, topic sentences, and lead sentences.

To create a detailed outline, writers substitute topic and lead sentences for the items of information in their sorting session.

Topic Sentences

Topic sentences overview the contents of paragraphs. A topic sentence begins a paragraph with the statement, "In order to sell commercial real estate, a broker must discuss three ideas with a prospective client." The rest of the paragraph describes the three ideas. When writers forecast information with a topic sentence, audiences read paragraphs quickly and intelligently.

Examples

- *This paragraph defines the concept of quality.*

- *Kendra Corporation opened its doors in 1955.*

- *We must solve the two-fold manufacturing process problem.*

- *Kendra solved the problem by examining three issues.*

Lead Sentences

Lead sentences are like topic sentences; they too overview paragraphs, but also "lure" audiences with their added appeal. Lead sentences take the form of questions, statistics, quotations, and stories that challenge, interest, and persuade audiences.

Examples

- *Should Congress pass a bill eliminating personal income tax?*

- *Sixty-five percent of the electorate favors eliminating personal income tax.*

- *Speaker of the House William Andrews has said, "The national debt has mired America in a ditch from which it may never emerge."*

- *At the same meeting, John Smith criticized Darrell Jones's point of view, sealing the defeat of the motion.*

Writing Style for Topic and Lead Sentences

Writers should use a clear, concise style in their memos. The following sentence contains four writing style problems that undermine effective writing.

> *It is obvious that this document will have to be amended from time to time as new duties arise and as present duties are altered in one fashion or another.*

Problem 1: the sentence is too long.

Problem 2: the writer failed to begin the sentence with a performing subject.

Problem 3: the writer failed to use concrete verbs.

Problem 4: the writer failed to use only necessary words.

In solving the four problems, the original sentence becomes

> *We will amend this document as duties change.*

Solution 1: Shorten the Sentence

The original sentence length forces audiences to retrace their steps even if the writer had constructed the original sentence well. Audiences should read sentences, not decipher them. As a rule, state one idea, and then place a period, as in the improved sentence.

Examples **Shorter Sentences**

- (Longer) *Real estate is booming in Las Vegas because of the influx of home buyers from California, and, of course, prices of single homes spiral ever upward.* (Shorter) *Real estate is booming in*

Las Vegas because of the influx of California home buyers. As a result, prices of single homes spiral upward.

- (Longer) *Certain institutions may loan money at high interest rates; however, laws preclude banks from doing so, and banks seek to balance this inequity.* (Shorter) *Certain institutions may loan money at exorbitant interest rates. However, laws preclude banks from doing so, and banks seek to balance this inequity.*

Solution 2: Start the Sentence With a Performing Subject

In the improved sentence, *We will amend this document as duties change*, "we" is the acting subject. By beginning sentences with a subject that acts, writers ensure sentences

1) Are shorter

2) Place meaning closer to the front of the sentence

3) Use concrete verbs rather than abstract ones.

Before beginning to write sentences, writers should list the performing subjects which will appear in the information they present. For each sentence they write, writers "plug in" a performing subject at the beginning of each sentence. A list of performing subjects might contain the names of

1) companies
2) customers
3) systems
4) processes
5) products
6) services

Examples   <u>**Performing Subjects (Underlined)**</u>

- *<u>Kendra Corporation</u> rejected their proposal.*

- *<u>Elaine Danvers, our communications expert,</u> presented a paper on the use of video conferencing technology.*

- *<u>The course development process</u> describes seven steps for instructional designers to follow.*

Solution 3: Follow the Performing Subject With a Concrete Verb

Concrete verbs like *demonstrate, test, develop, initiate, validate,* and *cooperate*—rather than weak/abstract verbs like *is, was, were, make, have, do,* and *give*—create images in audiences' minds and enhance their ability to comprehend quickly and thoroughly. Concrete verbs are powerful words that condense meaning and negate the need for excessive supporting language.

Examples   <u>**Concrete Verbs (Underlined)**</u>

- *Kendra Corporation <u>rejected</u> their proposal.*

- *Elaine Danvers, our communications expert, <u>presented</u> a paper on the use of video conferencing technology.*

- *The course development process <u>describes</u> seven steps for instructional designers to follow.*

Solution 4: Use Necessary Words Only

The writer of the original sentence, *It is obvious that this document will have to be amended from time to time as new duties are altered in one fashion or another,* used unnecessary words. He or she should have verified the need for all forms of *that, which, shall, will, would, could, should, had,* and also words ending in *-ly*. The writer should have deleted meaningless phrases like *it is obvious, from time to time,* and *in one fashion or another.* Writers become infatuated with a padded style, believing that "more is better" rather than "less is more."

Unnecessary Words

Examples

- *In today's modern world* (Today)

- *A large segment of the population* (Many)

- *The purpose of this memo is to describe...* (This memo describes)

- *The team gave consideration to the features of the product* (The team considered the product's features)

- *Obviously* (delete word—if it's obvious, the audience will know that)

- *I believe* (delete phrase—of course you believe, you are the writer)

- *I feel* (delete phrase—same rationale as *I believe*)

Sample

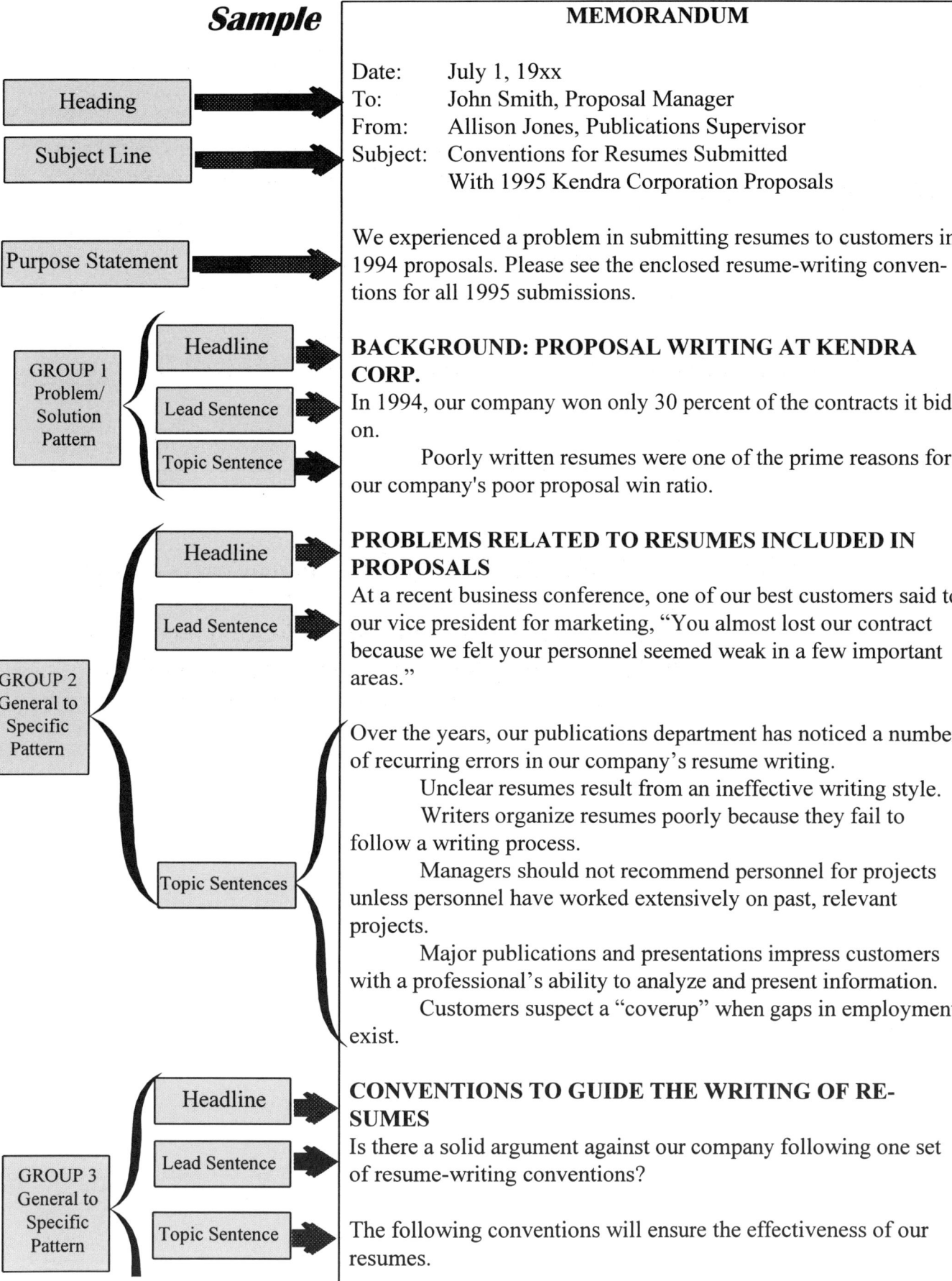

MEMORANDUM

Date: July 1, 19xx
To: John Smith, Proposal Manager
From: Allison Jones, Publications Supervisor
Subject: Conventions for Resumes Submitted
            With 1995 Kendra Corporation Proposals

We experienced a problem in submitting resumes to customers in 1994 proposals. Please see the enclosed resume-writing conventions for all 1995 submissions.

BACKGROUND: PROPOSAL WRITING AT KENDRA CORP.
In 1994, our company won only 30 percent of the contracts it bid on.
        Poorly written resumes were one of the prime reasons for our company's poor proposal win ratio.

PROBLEMS RELATED TO RESUMES INCLUDED IN PROPOSALS
At a recent business conference, one of our best customers said to our vice president for marketing, "You almost lost our contract because we felt your personnel seemed weak in a few important areas."

Over the years, our publications department has noticed a number of recurring errors in our company's resume writing.
        Unclear resumes result from an ineffective writing style.
        Writers organize resumes poorly because they fail to follow a writing process.
        Managers should not recommend personnel for projects unless personnel have worked extensively on past, relevant projects.
        Major publications and presentations impress customers with a professional's ability to analyze and present information.
        Customers suspect a "coverup" when gaps in employment exist.

CONVENTIONS TO GUIDE THE WRITING OF RESUMES
Is there a solid argument against our company following one set of resume-writing conventions?

The following conventions will ensure the effectiveness of our resumes.

Heading

Subject Line

Purpose Statement

GROUP 1
Problem/
Solution
Pattern

Headline

Lead Sentence

Topic Sentence

GROUP 2
General to
Specific
Pattern

Headline

Lead Sentence

Topic Sentences

GROUP 3
General to
Specific
Pattern

Headline

Lead Sentence

Topic Sentence

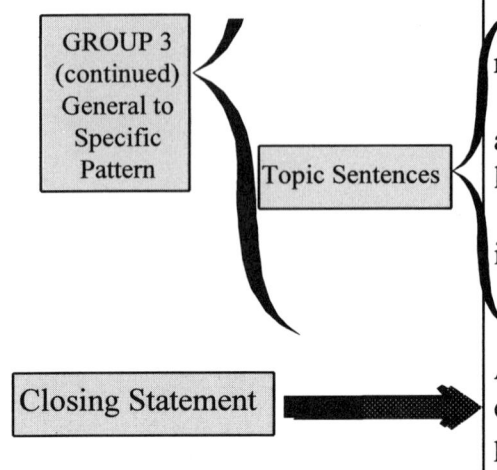

GROUP 3 (continued) General to Specific Pattern

Topic Sentences

> A telegraphic writing style ensures the conciseness of our resumes
>
> Writers should use all caps for first level heads, initial caps and underlining for second level heads, and initial caps for third level heads.
>
> Writers should paginate resumes and verify that pages are in order before stapling.
>
> Writers should not abbreviate dates, addresses, and the like.

Closing Statement

> At each proposal kick-off meeting, please distribute copies of the enclosed resume-writing conventions to all proposal writers and project personnel.

Action Use **_Power Tool #3-Outline View_** on pages 45-46 to substitute topic and lead sentences for items of information in the sorting session (**_Step 10-Sort_**). This means that a detailed outline will contain a topic or lead sentence for each paragraph of the memo's first draft.

STEP 12. FIRST DRAFT

Principle   To write a first draft, writers expand the topic and lead sentences of the detailed outline into paragraphs. This expanding occurs by adding sentences that amplify the meaning of topic and lead sentences, and using the same writing style discussed in Step 11 (Writing Style for Topic and Lead Sentences, pages 59-62).

To expand topic and lead sentences, writers should:

1. Begin anywhere in the outline, at the easiest section to write

2. Explain ideas to a friend or colleague (real or imagined) to achieve a conversational tone so that ideas flow

3. Write, not revise. Save revising for the last step in the memo writing process.

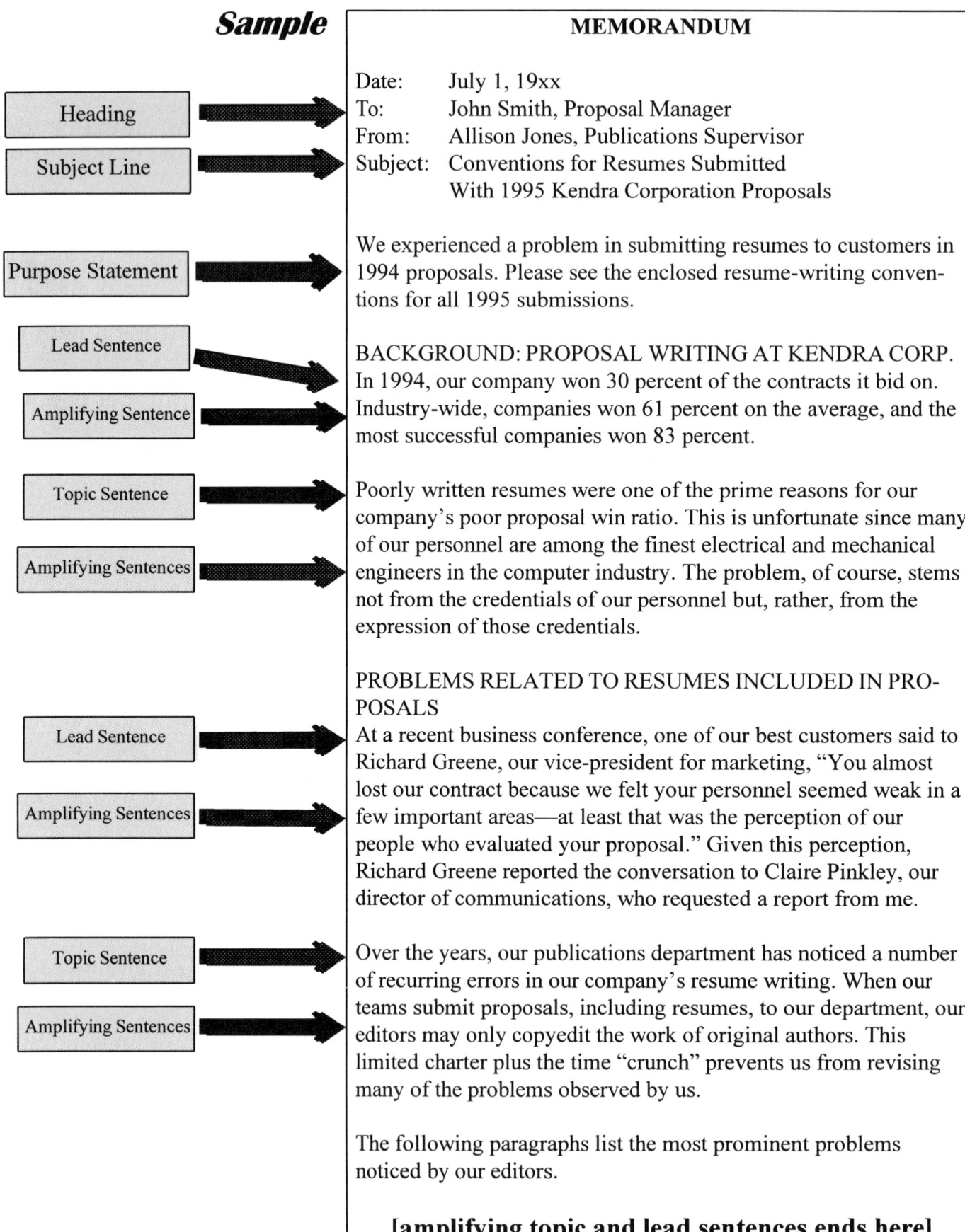

Sample

Heading ➡

Subject Line ➡

Purpose Statement ➡

Lead Sentence ➡

Amplifying Sentence ➡

Topic Sentence ➡

Amplifying Sentences ➡

Lead Sentence ➡

Amplifying Sentences ➡

Topic Sentence ➡

Amplifying Sentences ➡

MEMORANDUM

Date: July 1, 19xx
To: John Smith, Proposal Manager
From: Allison Jones, Publications Supervisor
Subject: Conventions for Resumes Submitted
          With 1995 Kendra Corporation Proposals

We experienced a problem in submitting resumes to customers in 1994 proposals. Please see the enclosed resume-writing conventions for all 1995 submissions.

BACKGROUND: PROPOSAL WRITING AT KENDRA CORP.
In 1994, our company won 30 percent of the contracts it bid on. Industry-wide, companies won 61 percent on the average, and the most successful companies won 83 percent.

Poorly written resumes were one of the prime reasons for our company's poor proposal win ratio. This is unfortunate since many of our personnel are among the finest electrical and mechanical engineers in the computer industry. The problem, of course, stems not from the credentials of our personnel but, rather, from the expression of those credentials.

PROBLEMS RELATED TO RESUMES INCLUDED IN PRO-POSALS
At a recent business conference, one of our best customers said to Richard Greene, our vice-president for marketing, "You almost lost our contract because we felt your personnel seemed weak in a few important areas—at least that was the perception of our people who evaluated your proposal." Given this perception, Richard Greene reported the conversation to Claire Pinkley, our director of communications, who requested a report from me.

Over the years, our publications department has noticed a number of recurring errors in our company's resume writing. When our teams submit proposals, including resumes, to our department, our editors may only copyedit the work of original authors. This limited charter plus the time "crunch" prevents us from revising many of the problems observed by us.

The following paragraphs list the most prominent problems noticed by our editors.

[amplifying topic and lead sentences ends here]

Unclear resumes result from an ineffective writing style.

Writers organize resumes poorly because they fail to follow a writing process.

Managers should not recommend personnel for projects unless personnel have worked extensively on past, relevant projects.

Major publications and presentations impress customers with a professional's ability to analyze and present information.

Customers suspect a "coverup" when gaps in employment exist.

USE THESE CONVENTIONS TO GUIDE THE WRITING OF RESUMES

Is there a solid argument against our company following one set of resume-writing conventions?

The following conventions will ensure the effectiveness of our resumes.

A telegraphic writing style ensures the conciseness of our resumes

Writers should use all caps for first level heads, initial caps and underlining for second level heads, and initial caps for third level heads.

Writers should paginate resumes and verify that pages are in order before stapling.

Writers should not abbreviate dates, addresses, and the like.

At each proposal kick-off meeting, please distribute copies of the enclosed resume-writing conventions to all proposal writers and project personnel.

Closing Statement

Action   Write the first draft of a memo using **Power Tool #3- Outline View** on pages 45-46. This allows you to write and shift ideas more easily than writing and moving ideas in Normal View.

When you finish with the first draft and wish to view your work as it will appear on a printed page, convert from Outline View to Normal View by selecting **Normal** on the View Menu.

STEP 13. REVISE

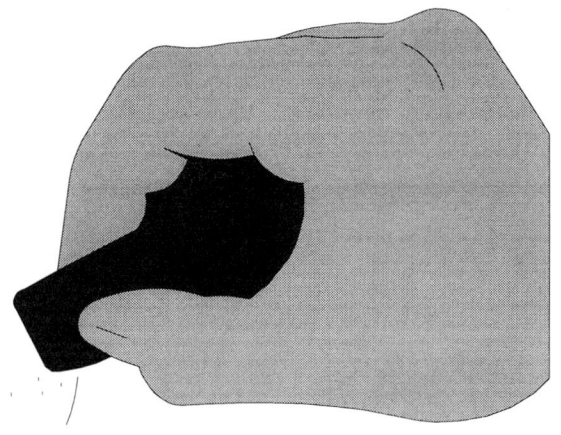

Principle Revising allows writers to correct passive voice; abstract verbs; unnecessary words; improper word usage; violations of grammar, punctuation, and capitalization rules.

Because writers have completed the first 12 steps of the memo writing process, revising will be minimal.

Sample

MEMORANDUM

Date: July 1, 19xx
To: John Smith, Proposal Manager
From: Allison Jones, Publications Supervisor
Subject: Conventions for Resumes Submitted
          With 1995 Kendra Corporation Proposals

We experienced a problem in submitting resumes to customers in 1994 proposals. Please see the enclosed resume-writing conventions for all 1995 submissions.

BACKGROUND: PROPOSAL WRITING AT KENDRA CORP.
In 1994, our company won 30 percent of the contracts it bid on. Industry-wide, companies won 61 percent on the average, and the most successful companies won 83 percent.

Poorly written resumes were one of the prime reasons for our company's poor proposal win ratio. This is unfortunate since many of our personnel are among the finest electrical and mechanical engineers in the computer industry. The problem, of course, stems not from the credentials of our personnel but, rather, from the expression of those credentials.

PROBLEMS RELATED TO RESUMES INCLUDED IN PRO-POSALS
At a recent business conference, one of our best customers said to Richard Greene, our vice-president for marketing, "You almost lost our contract because we felt your personnel seemed weak in a few important areas—at least that was the perception of our people who evaluated your proposal." Given this perception, Richard Greene reported the conversation to Claire Pinkley, our director of communications, who requested a report from me.

Over the years, our publications department has noticed a number of recurring errors in our company's resume writing. When our teams submit proposals, including resumes, to our department, our editors may only copyedit the work of original authors. This limited charter plus the time "crunch" prevents us from revising many of the problems observed by us.

The following paragraphs list the most prominent problems noticed by our editors.

[amplifying topic and lead sentences ends here]
[correcting grammar and style ends here, too]

Annotations (in margin boxes):

- Unnecessary Word
- Violates rule: don't end sentence with preposition
- Abstract Verbs
- Unnecessary Words
- Violates rule: Capitalize titles
- Unnecessary Word
- Passive Voice

70

Unclear resumes result from an ineffective writing style.

Writers organize resumes poorly because they fail to follow a writing process.

Managers should not recommend personnel for projects unless personnel have worked extensively on past, relevant projects.

Major publications and presentations impress customers with a professional's ability to analyze and present information.

Customers suspect a "coverup" when gaps in employment exist.

USE THESE CONVENTIONS TO GUIDE THE WRITING OF RESUMES

Is there a solid argument against our company following one set of resume-writing conventions?

The following conventions will ensure the effectiveness of our resumes.

A telegraphic writing style ensures the conciseness of our resumes

Writers should use all caps for first level heads, initial caps and underlining for second level heads, and initial caps for third level heads.

Writers should paginate resumes and verify that pages are in order before stapling.

Writers should not abbreviate dates, addresses, and the like.

Closing Statement →

At each proposal kick-off meeting, please distribute copies of the enclosed resume-writing conventions to all proposal writers and project personnel.

Action Use the following Power Tools to revise a memo:

Power Tool #4-Thesaurus on page 73 to substitute concrete verbs (and other words) for abstract ones.

Power Tool #5-Spell Check and Custom Dictionary on page 75 to find spelling errors and build a dictionary of commonly used but non-traditionally spelled words, jargon.

Power Tool #6-Grammar Check on page 77 to correct violations of grammatical rules. Grammar Check also verifies a memo's readability level.

Power Tool #7-Word Count on page 79 to verify the number of pages, words, characters, paragraphs, and lines in a memo.

Power Tool #8-Tables on pages 81-82 to convert text to a more readily understandable tabular format.

POWER TOOL #4
THESAURUS

WORD's Thesaurus tool helps writers choose concrete verbs and other image-producing words to invigorate sentences. The Thesaurus tool is an on-screen version of the familiar standard reference book.

1. Place your cursor on the word you wish to replace. Click on **Tools - Thesaurus**.

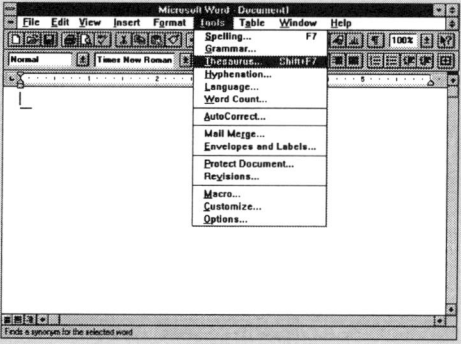

A dialog box appears:

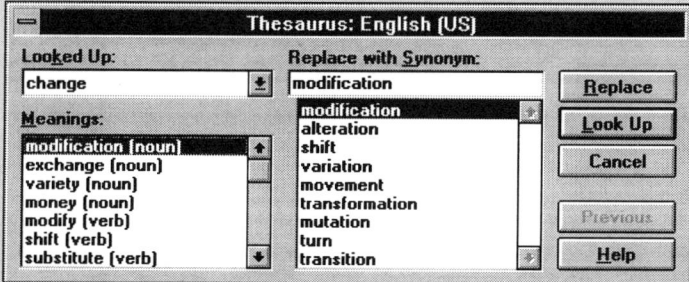

The word your cursor was on appears in the **Looked Up** box.

2. In **Meanings**, click on the appropriate denotation of your **Looked Up** word. Clicking on the denotation will highlight the word and show synonyms in the **Replace With Synonym** section.

3. In **Replace With Synonym**, click on the synonym of choice.

4. Click the **Replace** button to select the highlighted synonym.

> **NOTE:** *Click on a highlighted word in* **Replace With Synonym** *and Thesaurus places the word in* **Looked Up,** *and displays corresponding synonyms in* **Replace With Synonym.**

POWER TOOL #5
SPELL CHECK and
CUSTOM DICTIONARY

WORD automatically checks the entire document for spelling errors unless you select only a specific area by highlighting that area.

1. Click on the **Spell Check** icon on the toolbar **or** click on **Tools - Spelling**.

When WORD comes to a word it doesn't recognize, it will highlight the word in the text and offer suggestions for replacement.

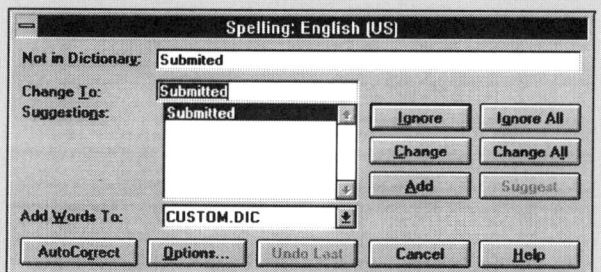

The unrecognized word appears in the **Not In Dictionary** box. **Change To** shows WORD's primary suggestion for replacement. **Suggestions** lists other alternatives for replacement.

2. Click on the **Change** button to change the unrecognized word to the one in the **Change To** box. To correct the same misspelling throughout the document, click on the **Change All** button.

3. To use one of the alternative suggestions, click on that word, causing it to appear in the **Change To** box. Then click on the **Change** or **Change All** button.

4. Spell Check also pauses on double words ("he walked <u>in in</u> his red shoes"), words that contain numbers ("2nd"), and words that have odd capitalization ("CompUSA").

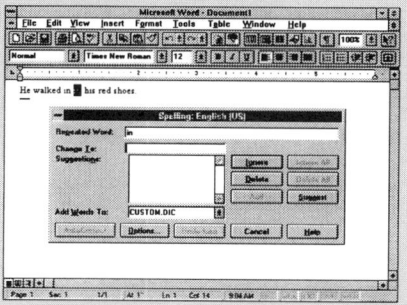

Spell Check is not a substitute for proofreading! It will not fix incorrect word usage, such as "there" instead of "their," nor will it catch single-letter word mistakes, such as "s" instead of "a."

Custom Dictionary

If the unrecognized word (or acronym) is spelled correctly but isn't recognized by WORD (many proper names fall into this category), clicking on **Add** will add it to WORD's dictionary to speed up the spell check process in the future.

*NOTE: Clicking on **Auto Correct** will cause WORD to correct the word every time you type it in the future. For example, if you chronically type "t e h" instead of "t h e," every time you type "t e h," WORD will automatically replace it with "t h e," often without you ever noticing. See page 21 for further tips about, and pitfalls of, **Auto Correct**.*

POWER TOOL #6
GRAMMAR CHECK

The Grammar Check tool is one of the most powerful, but least used of all the tools available in WORD. It is also a very easy tool to use.

1. After you have written your document, click on **Tools - Grammar** to begin the grammar check.

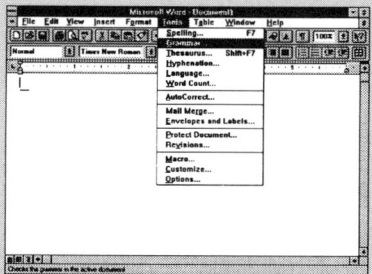

> **NOTE:** *When you use Grammar Check, WORD will also check the document's spelling, so there is no need to run a separate Spell Check.*

2. The Grammar Check dialog box looks like this:

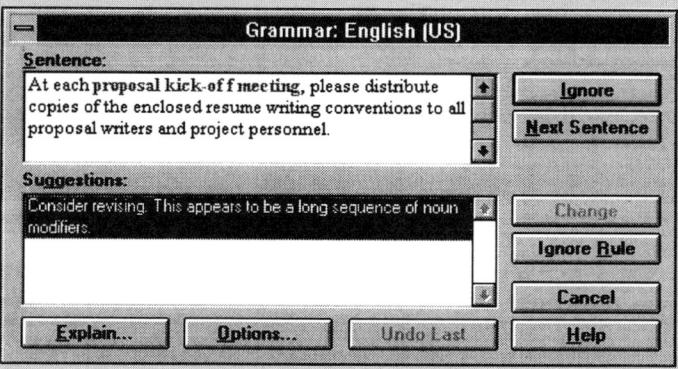

The **Sentence** box contains the sentence in question, sometimes with a specific group of words highlighted. Be aware, though, that **Sentence** does not always highlight faulty words.

Suggestions explains what WORD thinks may be wrong with the sentence, and offers a correction.

3. To see a further explanation of the suggestion and/or the rule invoked, click on **Explain**.

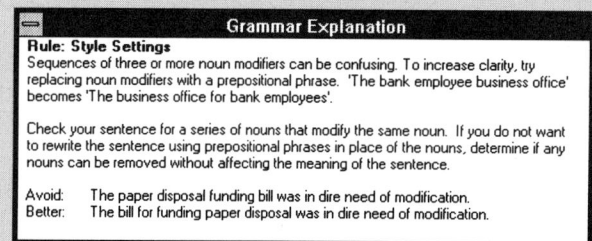

4. Clicking on the **Ignore** button skips the particular problem in the sentence.

5. Next Sentence instructs WORD to skip to the next sentence in which it detects a problem.

6. Change automatically makes the suggested change in the sentence.

7. Ignore Rule will skip subsequent occurrences of the same error in the document.

8. At the end of Grammar Check, WORD displays a box entitled **Readability Statistics**, which displays valuable information about the reader-friendliness of your document. It shows the average length of words and sentences, gives a reading ease percentage (the closer to 100%, the better), and tells what grade level the reader must have mastered to grasp the information.

POWER TOOL #7
WORD COUNT

The Word Count tool is useful for documents required to be a specific word length or number of pages. This is an especially valuable tool in these days of page-constrained memos, reports, and proposals—when many writers must squeeze e-mail and other documents within the boundaries of a computer screen.

1. Click on **Tools - Word Count**.

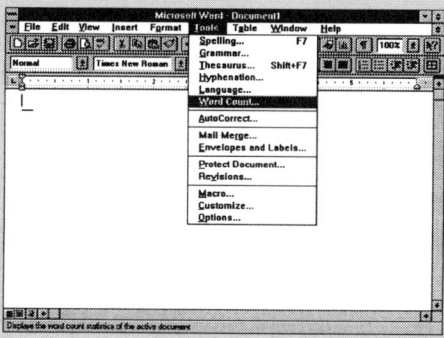

You will see important statistics about your document displayed.

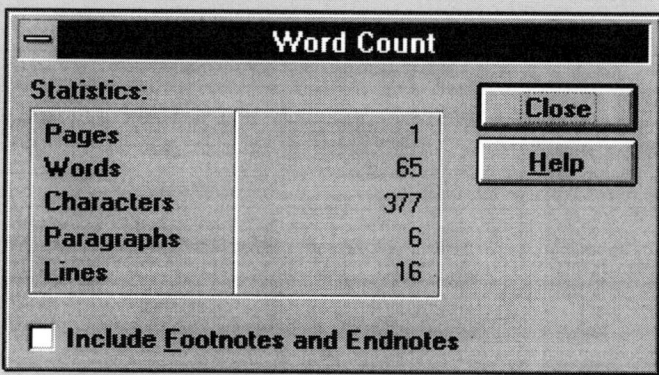

2. Click on **Include Footnotes and Endnotes** if you want them included in the count.

POWER TOOL #8
TABLES

Tables serve important functions for audiences and writers. For audiences, they

- *Quickly show relationships among data and ideas*
- *Save reading time by omitting repetitious text, and condensing the amount of information to remember*

For writers, tables

- *Display mistakenly omitted information and poor organization*

Constructing a table is a simple process. Decide how many rows (horizontal) and columns (vertical) you need.

1. With your cursor at the point where you want the table inserted, click on the **Insert Table** icon on the toolbar.

A 4 x 5 square grid will appear on the screen, with Cancel at the bottom.

Start with the upper left square in the grid. Using the left mouse button, click and drag the arrow across the grid until the grid highlights the number of columns and rows your table needs.

Don't be alarmed if the initial on-screen grid contains too few rows and/or columns. They will increase as you drag the arrow. When you release the mouse button, the table with the desired number of rows and columns will appear on your screen.

2. Type normally inside each cell, and use formatting options (i.e., bold, justification, italics) just as you would in normal text.

3. (A) To adjust the appearance of the table or "make it pretty," click on **Table - Table Auto Format**. WORD has several pre-set table formatting options available.

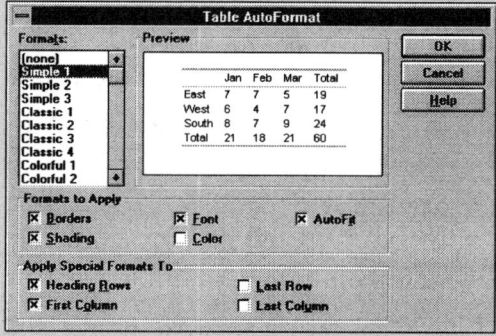

Click on each option to view a sample. You may also apply or cancel specific options—such as font, borders, and shading—in this dialog box.

(B) To adjust borders, gridlines, and shading manually within a table, click on the **Borders** icon on the Formatting toolbar (located on the far right, beneath the Help icon).

The Borders toolbar will appear. Click in the leftmost box to adjust the width and boldness of the border line you are about to apply. Place your cursor in the cell to be adjusted, or highlight a group of cells. Then click on any of the line options. The last line option will delete borders and gridlines.

Click in the far right box of the Borders toolbar to adjust shading within a cell or group of cells.

(C) Other adjustments you may want to make:

Add a row: Click on **Table - Insert Row.**

Delete a row: Highlight the row. Click on **Table - Delete Row,** or with your cursor in the row to delete, click on **Table - Delete Cells - Delete Entire Row**.

Add a column: Highlight the column to the right of the place you want to insert a new column. Click on **Table - Add Column**. The new column will be inserted to the left of the highlighted column. To add a column to the right of the table, place your cursor at the end of a table row outside the table. Click on **Table - Select Column**; then click on **Table - Insert Column**.

Delete a column: Highlight the column you want to delete. Click on **Table - Delete Column**, or with your cursor in the column to delete, click on **Table - Delete Cells - Delete Entire Column**.

Column Width: Find the column width symbol by rolling the mouse over the gridlines until the indicator appears. The indicator is two vertical lines flanked by right and left arrows.

Drag the column width symbol to the right or left to increase or decrease the width of columns.

INDEX

A

Audience 23
Auto Correct 21, 75

B

Brainstorm 41, 42

C

Chronological pattern 52
Classify 43, 44
Closing statement 39, 40, 42
Comparison/contrast pattern 53
Concrete verbs 61, 72, 73
Constructive tone 30
Custom Dictionary 72, 75

D

Demote button, in WORD 45
Demote To Body Text button, in WORD 45
Detailed outline 57, 64, 65

F

Firm tone 30
First draft 65, 67
First Line Only button, in WORD 46
Footer, in memos 18
Formal tone 30, 31
Format 15, 19

G

General to specific pattern 52
Grammar Check 72, 77

H

Header, in memos 18
Heading, memo 17, 19, 33
Heading Numbering, in WORD 46
Headlines 47, 49

INDEX

INDEX

R

Readability statistics 77
Reporting pattern 52
Revise 69

S

Separator line, in Memo Wizard 18
Show Formatting button, in WORD 46
Smart quotes 21
Sort 45, 51
   chronological pattern 52
   comparison/contrast pattern 53
   general to specific pattern 52
   most important to least important pattern 52
   problem/solution pattern 54
   spatial pattern 53
Spatial pattern 53
Spell Check 72, 75
Straight quotes 21
Subject line 33, 34

T

Table of Contents, in WORD 46
Tables 81
Thesaurus 72, 73
Tone 29
   constructive tone 30
   firm tone 30
   formal tone 30, 31
   informal tone 30
   informative tone 31
   motivating tone 39
Topic sentence 58, 64, 65

U

Unnecessary words 62

W

Word Count 79
Writing style 59